D1430761

Under the Crimson Sky

Neha Taneja

PARTRIDGE

To order additional copies of this book, contact
Partridge India
000 800 10062 62
orders.india@partridgepublishing.com

www.partridgepublishing.com/india

Under the Crimson Sky

Neha Taneja

PARTRIDGE

To order additional copies of this book, contact
Partridge India
000 800 10062 62
orders.india@partridgepublishing.com

www.partridgepublishing.com/india

Contents

Thoughts

Thoughts before meeting her:
Should I take a rose?
Or read a love prose.
Or simply take her for a walk
on a woodland road.

Moonlit Boulevard

Sepia shadows walked in
the moonlit boulevard
Sensual love was made.
Dream was broken by the
vintage velvet sheets
Which she had clutched.

Kohl Rimmed Eyes

She swayed into the ballroom
wearing red heels
Her kohl rimmed eyes met his.
Followed his lead swirled in passion
Bold moves burned the floor.

Desolate House

Once upon a time the melody
of romance filled the air
The fragrance of flowers
led her to his liar.
Love stung they were, Weeks
slipped into months.
Now the desolate house is surrounded,
by The forgotten garden.

Same Roads

The same roads we walked together
Same things we talked.
Neither knew that time would slip away
Never to meet again.
Took the same road again
Only to notice times have changed.
Vigorous climbers cover the path
leaving it to be discovered again.

Starry Night

Lying beside you on a shimmery night
Counting the diamonds till
sleep filled our eyes.
Don't want the sun to arise
To ruin the perfect night.

Mountains and the Moors

Across the mountains and the moors
All of the bridges are burnt
Reaching out till I find you
to the end of the road.

Crimson Dreamscape

Far from the mundane life
Where no one can watch us.
We steal moments together
And dance on the rhythm of love.
In the crimson dreamscape
Our only unbothered escape.

Walk With Me Forever

Promise to walk along
Uphill along winding paths.
Walk with me forever into light or dark.

Last Tea

Remenents of the last tea
Dried flowers, Neruda,
letters and love quotes
Only treasure of old love.

I Am Yours

Beneath the flowery boughs
Where the twilight tip toes
To kiss the ground
Was waiting for her
To say 'I am yours'.

Handkerchiefs

Handkerchiefs of his
Lay in the drawer of my closet
All stolen during the lovely visits
My secret dirty addiction.

In the Parallel World

Waiting by the brook
My love knows no rush
With the brush of fate will
meet you anywhere
Even in the parallel world.

Old Tin Box

Old tin box
Held memories together
Perfumed letters of his.

In My Dreams

She tip toed from behind
And covered my eyes.
All I wanted was to turn
around and kiss.
The alarm rang, woke up and realized
It all happened in my dreams.

Glimpse of Yours

Walking along noticed
you sipping coffee,
Lost in your own chaos.
Now walk by everyday to
catch a glimpse of yours.

No Matter

No matter where you are
Will reach out to you
From the darkest dungeons
To the deepest oceans
I will crawl to you.

Meteor

Like a meteor came your love
Fast and engulfing lighting
my entire universe
But short lived it was.

Love in Library

Met you in the library
Eyes met across the hall.
Love confession was needed
So looking for quotes that's all.
Keats, Shelly and Wordsworth
All were there
But I was lost behind words.

Message in a Bottle

Left a message in a bottle
That could reach him
Across the seas
Wishing it returns with
A message saying
Love returned and received.

Wrap Your Love

When you wrap your love
The joy it brings
Soothes my soul like a balm.
The tight brace against your chest
Can only calm.

Sign of Love

On a car ride
By the roadside
See the beds of flowers
Some bloomed
Some about to
Sign of love
The fields of hope.

Bitter Loving Grip

Reading through your letters
Finding the words of love
Burn them one by one
And gradually feel out of love.
To rescue me from your
Bitter loving grip
Had to let go every part of you.

Captivating Smile

Captivating smile of yours
The killing smile of yours
Wish to meet again.
But Where?
Chances are at the bar
Where you captured my heart.

Our Story

Our story of joy
Sorrows and pain.
Our story never to told again.
Only to be found in the pages
Of book of love of mine.

Love Followed the Way

Sunset on the beach
Can't figure out how to say.
With the brush of hands
It became easy
Love followed the way.

Reminded Me of You

It rained and the flowers bloomed
The rain soaked petals
Reminded me of you.
The bouquets, walks and conversations
Which were now without you.

Curious Crimson Sun

The curious crimson sun
Before it bids us night
Wants to know the stories
Of all lovers waiting by the riverside.

Casting Shadows of Love

Along the yellow grass
Casting shadows of love
Walked a couple
Hand in hand.

Signs of You

Years of memories gathered
in the suitcase
Signs of you remain here
Postcards with frayed bends
Love notes where the love ends.

Beauty of the Day

Beauty of the day
Strutted across the
Parking lot.
Eyes with emotions
Gazing at the street.
Vougish she dressed
To slay the hearts around.
I am still looking for her
but she is nowhere to be found.

Puzzle to Your Heart

Thought it to be a piece of art
But it was a puzzle you had left for me.
Took me a while to figure out
How the different passages
lead to your heart.
The enigma is indeed a
clever proposal art.

Love in Dandelion Field

In a field full of dandelions
Hope to meet you again
Like the old times
When you blew them
Off their stems.
I would make a wish
Hoping it would come true
The wish to be forever with you.

Secret Code of Love

Leaving notes as trail
To lead me to you
Favourite way of yours.
Sometimes leaving a scarf
Was a secret code of love.

Will Wait for You

Beyond the same old stream
Beneath the bougainvillea shade
Will wait for you
Every day at the same time
Hoping we would meet again.

Love

We met as buds
With love in our hearts
Then we bloomed
So did the love
Now we are flowers
In life's garden.

In Winding Lanes

It's been a long journey
In the winding lanes
With myriad colours
Looking for that balcony
Where you stood
And waved at me.

Last Evening

Last evening you just walked in
It was an unremembered thing
Which you always did
Long time back.
Emerged a crisp new day
Next to me curled up you lay
Your shoulder my refuge.

Old Phone Text

In the haphazard grid
Of life where I stand now.
I am occasionally alive
When I read your old text.
It keeps the faith intact
That you would call tonight.

Pain and Love

She lives here
In my heart
She is both
Pain and love.

Date Night

Date night it was
Black dress and pink lipstick
Eagerness in hazel eyes.
Tracing fingers on the glass rim
Only she thought of him.
With every breath she took
She remembered him.
There he was with the flowers
And the ring.

Love in Post-Its

No worries and take care
Post-Its which I leave around
Have deeper meaning.
Read in between the lines
Reminding you always
Am there always
Waiting for you.

Shooting Star

In a sky full of stars
Spotted a shooting star
Made a wish to meet again.
Here we stand
on the boughs of time
fated to love.

Cobbled Path

The yellow green grass
In between lay the cobbled path
Leading to the home on the bay.
The sunrise and the sunset
Adding colours each day.

Camouflaged Life

With a smile on the face
And pain in the eyes.
He would weep in the Rain
To hide his tears.

Power of Woman

She wore her scars
Like medals
And walked with elan
On undulating paths.

Goodbye

Entwining fingers
Eyes saying it all
Its time that we part.
No promised tomorrow's
Thy love brings the sorrow
Alas! We part to say goodbye.

Empty Cauldron

Heart is empty like the cauldron
With the walls scathed of
Wounds of love sticking around.
No matter how many rains of love come
None can fill it and wash
The pain and wounds down.

Looking for Him

In the blindling sandstorm
She fought to walk
Covering the expanse of the desert
Looking for him.
It was a mirage she followed
And this was a dream.
She awoke feeling
The smoothness of the
Satin sheets on her skin.

Moonlit Night

On a moonlit night
When you held me close
Near the riverside.
With the violin tunes
Setting the mood right.
The glowworms too
Danced on symphony of love.

Stories of Love

In the storeroom
Inside a carton
Found old parchments
Inked with promises.
Tales like these
Are eternal stories
Of love.

Her Fragrance

The wind distilled
with her distinct fragrance
reminded him of
those intimate moments
when he would
say her name.

Bitter East Wind

Suddenly entered my life
And turned it topsy-turvy
A bitter east wind.
Swept away the last
Remains of you.

Mind of a Woman

Cublicles of her mind had space
For love, warmth and joy.
Pain stayed for her lonely days
When the rest of the world rejoiced.

Strength of a Woman

She carries the world
On her shoulders
While dancing
On tunes of life
Carefully trudging
On the slippery paths of life.

Petrichor

Signs of rain
Petrichor filling the senses
Memories of our love
Fanned by the restless wind.

The Tempest

He had no plans for love
But she arrived
Breathtaking and beautiful
This tempest contained
The best laid plans
He gave in.

Hook of Love

The deal of love
Was sealed with promises
To stay together
Sign was the clasping fingers
Symbol of hook of love.

Their Spot

Pacing fast
Along the stony path
Hoping for that love gain
Looking at the watch
Now and then.
Across the river bend
She stood waving at him
Their spot where they had parted ways.

© Amrita Ghanty

Wrinkles

Wrinkles of experience traced the face
Strands of wisdom added grace
Blurring vision traversed high and low
Left with stories, and
everything to let go.

Lakes of Broken Love

Unstoppable rain of tears
Filled lakes of broken love
Depths couldn't be measured
Deeper than the skies above.

Love in Books

Marigolds and Rose
Love songs and prose
Yellowed with time
Lay pressed in a book
Last Chapter of Mine.

Desolate House

Sparse grass colored leaves
Torn curtains with peeping scenes
Desolate house of unfulfilled dreams.

Sibling Love

Find me behind the old trunk
Find me behind the bushes and trees
Find me beneath the sheets on the bunk.

Quest for Love

On a quest for love
Travelled to the last corner
Love was in the journey
from there and back
Carried bits of love from
everywhere in my back pack.

Lonely Forests

Walked for miles
Stumbling upon the bushes
And thorns.
Never stopping to look behind
Following the narrow
Paths of the lonely forests.

Same Bushes and Trees

Same bushes and trees
Where we played as children
And ran wild and free.
Paths we follow
Are different now
Leading to divergent
bushes and trees.

Noel Foning

Golden Bye

Peeping through the bushes
Waving a golden bye.
With promises to return
Beckoning the night sky.

Thoughts of a Payphone

Thoughts of a Payphone
When was last the town painted red?
When was last a lover visited?
Felt the heartbeats of millions
Now the love is lost in
messages and emoticons.

Noel Jeming

Wrinkles of Wisdom

Greys of time
Spreading warmth and peace
Which don't cost a dime.

9 781543 702828